Air Fryer Cookbook

The Simple Guide To Air Frying For Smart People – Air Fryer Recipes – Clean Eating

Air Fryer Cookbook

of information contained within this document, including, but not limited to, —errors, omissions, or inaccuracies.

Table of Contents

Introduction

Health is wealth and it is extremely important for you to pay attention to what you add to your body. In order to stave off illnesses, it is vital to incorporate clean and healthy food items in your diet, But hectic lifestyles and time crunches cause even the most fervent health junkie to end up settling for fried and junk foods on a routine basis. I'm sure you too satisfy your craving every now and then and end up going on a guilt trip.

However, thanks to the wonders of an Air Fryer, you don't have to feel guilty about satisfying your cravings anymore. An air fryer is a unique cooking utensil that can be used to cook healthy foods without having to worry about consuming unhealthy fats. The air fryer is a unique device that is easy to use and aids in cooking nutritional food.

In this book, we will look at the key aspects of an air fryer, why your kitchen needs one to have one, and also simple recipes you can prepare using your air fryer.

Let's get started!

Chapter 1: What is an Air Fryer?

First and foremost, I wish to thank you for choosing this book and hope you have a good time reading it.

In this first chapter, we will look at the meaning of an air fryer.

What is an air fryer?

I'm sure you have come across television ads and infomercials showcasing people using an air fryer, and wondered what it is all about. Well, as the name suggests, an air fryer is a device that makes use of air to cook foods.

It basically works by circulating hot air around the food thereby cooking it effectively. It makes use of a fan that produces and circulates the air around the food.

Maillard reaction

The Maillard reaction is a chemical reaction that takes place between amino acids and sugars that causes foods to develop a unique taste. It also causes baked foods to develop their distinct brown color.

The air fryer makes use of the same technology and causes the amino acids and sugar in the foods to react and develop a brown color.

The mechanism makes the food crispy on the outside, thereby giving it the feeling of a baked or fried food item.

The air fryer is capable of raising the air temperature to up to 200 degree Celsius, which means it permeates through the food to cook it thoroughly.

Here are the different things you can do with an air fryer.

Roasting

This is the most used function of the air fryer. It will be extremely easy for you to roast your foods as the air fryer works very fast. All you have to do is prepare the vegetables or meats by cutting them into small pieces and then add them to the roasting attachment. You don't have to worry about turning or moving them around, as the air fryer will do all the work for you. The air fryer takes 20% lesser time to roast your vegetables and meats, which makes it great for bachelors, and those in a hurry to cook their food.

Frying

Now you don't have to worry about deep-frying foods, as it is quite easy to use an air fryer to get the desired results. In fact, you don't need any oil at all to fry the foods, as the fryer makes use of hot air to crisp up foods. All you have to do is add in a little oil to the ingredient mix, which the air fryer will use to both cook and crisp the food. You can, however, brush a little oil on top to make it a little crunchier if you like.

Grilling

It is extremely easy to grill in an air fryer and you only have to expend a little effort towards it. You don't have to worry about constantly flipping the food, as all you have to do is add the food and wait. Once you reach the half way mark, you can give the fryer a gentle shake in order to readjust the food within it. You will have to use the grill attachment, as that will make it easy for you to move the food by using the handle attached to it. The shaking also helps with absorbing or draining the excess oil, thereby making the food healthier.

Baking

Baking is made extremely easy with the air fryer. You don't have to worry about not having a conventional oven, as the air fryer will work well for all your baking needs. It works on pretty much the same rules as an oven and you have to preheat it before baking. You can make cookies, biscuits, muffins, cupcakes etc. It only takes around 15 to 30 minutes and an entire batch will be ready. You have to use the special attachment that is provided for baking purposes. The results will be much better than what you might have with a microwave.

The meats that cook well in an air fryer include pork, chicken, beef and fish. The vegetables that roast well in an air fryer include pepper, kale, zucchini, cauliflower, asparagus and corn. Potatoes are the most commonly cooked vegetables in the air fryer.

You can simultaneously cook two or more foods at the same time, as your air fryer will come with a separator attachment. You can separate the meals using the separator and cook all at the same time.

Chapter 2: How Does The Air Fryer Work?

The air fryer is a convenient little device that can be used to cook food at a faster pace. Here is looking at the basic functioning of the air fryer.

Air fryer parts

The air fryer looks like a rice cooker, and comes with 3 distinct parts. The first part is the machine itself, which will work by generating hot air that cooks the food within the fryer. The second is the attachment that will carry the food item. The frying basket is the most commonly used attachment. You will also avail a basic pan and a baking tin. The third component is the container. The container holds on to all unwanted food residue such as oil and spices.

The front of the machine carries the temperature and timer that can be adjusted according to the food to be cooked. The insides of the main machine are made up of 5 distinct parts. The back of the machine comes with the water tank. The top of the machine has 4 parts starting with a heating element at the bottom followed by the heating fan, followed by the cooling fan and then the engine.

The main body of the machine might look a little different depending on the brand but most of them pretty much look the same from the inside.

Air fryer mechanism

The air fryer is a simple device that makes use of hot air to cook food. It is fairly simple for you to roast, bake or fry foods without having to rely on the conventional methods.

It has a fan that generates hot air. This hot air coats the ingredient and cooks it thoroughly. You don't have to worry about moving the food around, as the air fryer does the job for you.

The air fryer raises the temperature of the air to up to 200 degrees Celsius, which makes it easy for you to cook the food. Although this temperature is mostly used to cook hard foods such as meats and vegetables, it can also be used to cook other types of food faster.

Using an air fryer is quite simple and the following are the steps to adopt.

Step 1: The first step is to prepare the air fryer. For this, start by picking the right attachment to be used. You have to place the attachment the right way in order for the air fryer to work.

Step 2: Preheat the air fryer so that it reaches the right temperature for your food. You can look up the instructional manual provided with your machine to check which temperature suits what food the best. Generally speaking, meats and hard vegetables require the highest temperature to cook.

Step 3: Brush a little oil over the food and place it inside the attachment before fixing it on to the air fryer.

Step 4: Choose the right timing and wait patiently. Once done, you can serve the dish hot.

Choosing the right air fryer

There are now many varieties of air fryers available in the market and you can choose the right one based on the following criteria

Family size
I
f you have a large family then you must buy the largest available air fryer. The larger ones come with larger attachments, which will allow you to cook large amounts of food at once.

Use
Not all your cooking can be done in an air fryer and it is important for you to analyze the complete use of the device before making your choice. If you want it just to make snacks then you can choose a smaller model. But if you wish to roast, bake, and fry then you can look up a high-end model that will help you with all of these functions.

Budget

The next criterion to consider is the budget. If you are on a smaller budget, then you can pick the starting model. But if you are looking for a good quality air fryer that will last you a long time, then you can buy a higher end model that might cost you a bit more, but will be well worth it.

Most of the newer models come with a digital display as compared to a manual turn knob.

Cleaning and maintenance

It is important for you to clean the air fryer from time to time to ensure that it serves you for as long as possible. Here are the simple steps that you can adopt to clean and maintain the air fryer.

- To clean the cooking basket start by filling a large enough tub with hot water and detergent to generate thick foam.
- Place the attachment within it and allow it to soak for a while before using a brush to clean it thoroughly.
- But be careful so as to not scrub it using harsh brushes as they can leave behind scratches.
- The outside of an air fryer will not get as greasy as a conventional fryer. All you have to do is wipe it with a damp cloth and your fryer will be as good as new.
- You can dip the cloth in hot water if you wish to loosen a stain.
- If there is a tough stain then you can use a toothbrush dipped in salt to scrub over the stain.
- But make sure you don't use a steel mesh or a hard bristled toothbrush as they can leave behind scratches on the body of the machine.

- You must also clean the basket at the bottom that catches the residue. You must empty it as soon as you finish the cooking and pop it into the dishwasher to clean it or follow the same procedure as you would to clean the attachment.

Chapter 3: Benefits Of An Air Fryer Vs. Traditional Fryers

The air fryer is a handy little utensil that you can use in your kitchen but is it any better than your regular air fryer? Well, let's find out.

Health

One of the biggest advantages of using the air fryer is it helps in eliminating the use of fats and oils. Regular fryers require you to add in lots of oil, which can be quite bad for your health. The air fryer, on the other hand, makes use of just a little oil that is applied on the food item or added to the mix. So if you are looking to improve your health by making dietary modifications, then it is a must for you to buy, and use an air fryer.

Time

It takes very little time for the air fryer to cook the meal as compared to a traditional fryer. The air fryer works by cutting down on as much as 20% of the time thereby saving you an hour or so of cooking. This is a great feature for bachelors and people who are generally busy. You don't have to worry about having to order out owing to a time crunch. You can simply add the ingredients to the air fryer and it will be ready in no time at all.

Ease to use

The air fryer is very easy to use and you don't have to put in too much effort to operate it. You can use the instructional manual provided with the machine to see how to operate it or can also watch an online instructional video. Anybody can use the air fryer including children and elders. You can demonstrate it for them and supervise a couple of times. In fact, it is a lot safer to use than traditional air fryers, as there is no need to add lots of hot oil to it.

Effort

You have to expend only a little effort to cook with the air fryer. Your job is pretty much done once you prepare the vegetables and meats and add to the air fryer. You don't have to stir it around or sauté it. You can kick back and relax while your dish gets prepared. This is unlike a traditional air fryer where you have to keep an eye on the dish to make sure it's cooking properly and also keep stirring or lifting the deep fryer basket. As mentioned earlier, even children can use the air fryer to make a dish.

Nutrition

Another major advantage of using the air fryer is it maintains the nutritional value of the food. You don't have to worry about the process removing some of the vital nutrients such as vitamins as the technology helps in trapping them within the food. This makes it ideal for people looking to improve their health by consuming healthy nutritious foods. The air fryer is comparable to a crock-pot except it cooks extremely fast.

Cost effective

Since there is no need to make use of lots of oil and other ingredients, your meals will turn out to be quite cost effective. You will only require smaller quantities of the ingredients, as there will not be too much loss due to cooking. This is especially great for meats and vegetables with high water content such as spinach. This is not possible with a regular fryer, as it will shrink the vegetables and meats, which will require you to add in some more or start with a big batch. Once you start using the air fryer, you will have a good idea of how cost effective it really is.

Variety

It is possible for you to make a variety of dishes using the air fryer, unlike the traditional fryer, where the deep-frying is the only option. As was mentioned earlier, you can bake, roast, fry and also grill using the air fryer. You can simultaneously do two things at once by using the separator attachment. Depending on the mix and what you apply on the outside of the food, you can fry and bake at the same time. The separator will not allow the two flavors to mix, thereby allowing you to prepare two distinct dishes at once.

Maintenance

Maintaining the air fryer is extremely easy. You only have to detach the attachment pan, and wash it like you would wash any utensil. It is also dishwasher friendly so you can simply pop it into the washer and forget about it. The body of the machine can be wiped using a damp cloth and it will be as good as new. If there is any tough stain on it then you can make a mix of baking soda and water and scrub the stain away.

Price

Many people wonder if the air fryer will prove to be quite expensive. However, it will not cost any more than your regular deep fryer. You can avail a good discount on an online store like amazon.com. The air fryer will last you a long time making it worth every penny you spend on it. It will also help you save on time and effort, which makes it an extremely useful device to add to your kitchen.

These are just some of the benefits of the air fryer that score over that of the traditional fryer and are not limited to just these. Once you start using the air fryer you will get acquainted with its other uses.

Chapter 4: About Clean Eating And Whole Foods

The air fryer is a great device to use to cook healthy foods no doubt, but you must also focus on clean eating habits in order to maintain a fit and healthy body. Clean eating refers to consuming whole foods and eliminating processed foods as much as possible. The main idea is to clean your palate and consume foods that are capable of eliminating toxins from your body, and avoiding their build up as well.

Here are some tips you can follow to increase clean eating.

Vegetables

Vegetables are full of body friendly nutrients and increasing your intake, and aid in enhancing your immunity. Vegetables are also quite low in calories, which make them an ideal choice for those looking to reduce their weight. It is important for an adult to consume about 3 cups of vegetables a day to maintain a healthy and lean body. Green, leafy vegetables are great for the entire body as they are rich in several vital nutrients that are requisite for the upkeep of the body.

Fruits

Fruits are just as important as vegetables and it is vital for you to consume as much fresh fruit as possible. You can replace unhealthy snacks with fruits. Try to eat 5 differently colored fruits each day so you can avail a multitude of nutrients. It is best to consume seasonal fruits but if you wish to have a particular fruit all around the year then you can cut them up and freeze them. You can juice the fruits or cut them up and add to water to make fruit infused water.

White flour

It is extremely important for you to cut out as much white flour from your diet as possible. White flour does not contain any fiber, which makes it hard to digest. It can clog up your system and might also lead to constipation. It is important for you to consume as less white flour as possible and instead replace it with whole-wheat flour.

Saturated fat

Clean eating must incorporate the cutting down on saturated fats. It is not possible for you to cut down on fats completely and must instead try to consume healthy fats such as olive oil, canola oil etc. These are rich in omega 3 fatty acids, which is great for your heart.

Alcohol

Clean eating includes cutting out all forms of alcohol from your diet including beer, wine and other such alcoholic beverages. It is fine to have an occasional glass of wine at the dinner table, but drinking regularly might not do any good for your body. You can always replace alcohol with healthier options such as fruit juices and fruit infused water. You can cut up a few lemons and add to a jug of water to be consumed at regular intervals, throughout the day.

Sugars

Try to avoid sugary foods as much as possible and replace the sugar with honey instead. This can be in your morning tea or even the sweets you prepare. Honey is extremely nutritious and also lends the right amount of sweetness to the dish. You must avoid consuming sodas as much as possible and replace them with fruit juices. You must also avoid adding in artificial sweeteners as well as they can contain unwanted chemicals.

Salt intake

Although salt makes food taste extremely good, it is quite important to consume it in the right quantities. Eating too much salt will have an adverse effect on your health as it has the capacity to raise your blood pressure. You must limit it to just 2,300 mg of sodium per day and not anymore. It helps to cut out processed foods that are generally laden with salts. You can remove the bottle of salt from the table to avoid reaching for it during meal times. You can make your dish flavorful by replacing the salt with herbs and spices.

Meat

Although meat is a great source of protein, it is best to limit its intake. It is best to limit to 3 or 4 meals per week. Choose lean meats whose fat has been cut down as much as possible. Don't discard the bones of meats and use them to make bone broth. Bone broth is extremely nutritious and can help in strengthening your body. You can replace a meat dish with bone broth soup to increase your nutrient intake.

Supplements

You can always consume some natural supplements such as ginseng and Ashwagandha as they are good for your body's functioning. They can enhance your body's capacity to deal with everyday stress and maintain a fit and healthy interior and exterior.

Whole foods

Whole foods refer to those that have not been processed. Processed foods refer to those that have undergone processing to add in color, flavor, preservatives, sweetness etc. All of these chemicals can be quite bad for your body and consuming them on a regular basis can render you ill.

It is important for you to cut them out as much as possible in order to maintain a lean and fit body.

Whole foods include vegetables, fruits lentils, beans, wheat, honey, oats, barley, oils and dairy products. Anything that has not been processed in a factory will count as whole foods. It is important for you to buy your fruits and vegetables from an organic market, as they will carry the ones that have been grown in fields that don't make use of fertilizers and chemicals.

You must buy meats from farms that allow free ranging.

Make it a point to read labels of foods, to see if they have been processed. If the label says artificial color, flavor, preservatives, sugars or nature identical substances have been added in then it means the product is processed.

This includes biscuits, cakes, chips, soda, ice creams etc. Even if they say they have acquired the raw ingredients from organic farms, they will still contain chemicals that can be harmful for your health. Condiments such as sauces and canned curries are also processed.

Processed foods also include junk foods that can contain unsaturated fats and chemicals.

You can always prepare healthier options for all of these by making use of your air fryer. You can look up healthier recipes online and prepare them as per the instructions provided. This book will leave you with many healthy air fryer recipes to kick-start your journey.

Chapter 5: Air Fryer Breakfast Recipes

Cheese Omelet

Ingredients:

- 1 large onion, chopped
- 2 tablespoons cheddar cheese, grated
- 3 eggs
- 1/2 teaspoon soy sauce
- Salt to taste
- Pepper powder to taste
- Cooking spray

Method:

1. Whisk together eggs, salt, pepper, and soy sauce.
2. Spray a small pan, which fits inside the air fryer with cooking spray.
3. Add onions and spread it all over the pan and place the pan inside the air fryer.
4. Air fry at 180 degree C for 6-7 minutes or until onions are translucent.
5. Pour the beaten egg mixture all over the onions. Sprinkle cheese all over it.
6. Air fry for another 5-6 minutes or until the eggs are set.
7. Remove from the air fryer and serve with toasted multi grain bread.

Japanese Omelet

Ingredients:

- 1/2 cup fresh Shimeji mushrooms, sliced
- 2 eggs, whisked
- A handful sliced Japanese silken tofu
- 2 tablespoons onion, finely chopped
- 1 clove garlic, minced
- Salt to taste
- Pepper powder to taste
- Cooking spray

Method:

1. Spray the baking accessory with cooking spray. Spray well with cooking spray.
2. Add onions and garlic.
3. Air fry in a preheated air fryer at 180 degree C for 4 minutes.
4. Place tofu and mushrooms over the onions.
5. Add salt and pepper to eggs and whisk again. Pour over the tofu and mushrooms.
6. Air fry for another 20-25 minutes. Pierce with a toothpick a couple of times in between to check if the eggs are well cooked.

Eggs En Cocotte on Toast

Ingredients:

- 2 eggs
- 1 cup Taiwan sausages, chopped into small pieces
- 1/4 teaspoon maple syrup
- 1/4 teaspoon balsamic vinegar
- 1/2 teaspoon Italian seasoning
- 1/4 teaspoon salt or to taste
- 1/8 teaspoon black pepper powder or to taste
- 2 slices whole wheat bread
- 3 tablespoons cheddar cheese
- 4-6 slices tomatoes
- Cooking spray
- A little mayonnaise to serve

Method:

1. Spray the baking accessory or baking dish (which is smaller than air fryer) with cooking spray.
2. Place the bread slices at the bottom of the dish. Sprinkle sausages over the bread.
3. Lay tomato slices over it. Sprinkle cheese over the tomato layer.
4. Break the eggs over the cheese (you can also beat the eggs and add if you wish).
5. Drizzle vinegar and maple syrup over the eggs. Sprinkle Italian seasoning, salt, and pepper. If you like it cheesy, then sprinkle some more cheese on top.
6. Place the baking dish in the air fryer basket.

7. Bake in a preheated air fryer at 160 degree C for 10 minutes.
8. Remove from the air fryer. Dote with mayonnaise and serve.

Air Fried Bacon

Ingredients:

- Bacon as much as required, sliced

Method:

1. Place the bacon in the air fryer basket and place the basket in the air fryer.
2. Air fry in a preheated air fryer at 200 degree C for 8-10 minutes.

French Toast Sticks

Ingredients:

- 4 eggs, beaten
- 8 slices whole wheat bread
- 1/2 teaspoon ground cinnamon
- 1/8 teaspoon ground cloves
- 1/8 teaspoon salt
- 1/8 teaspoon ground nutmeg
- 4 tablespoons butter, softened
- Maple syrup to serve
- Cooking spray

Method:

1. Add salt, cinnamon, nutmeg, and cloves to beaten eggs and whisk lightly.
2. Apply butter on either side of the bread slices. Cut into strips of about 1 inch wide.
3. Dip each of the strips in the egg mixture and place in the preheated air fryer pan. Air fry at 180 degree C for about 6 -7 minutes. Place as many as you can but do not crowd. You can cook in batches.
4. After about 2 minutes of air frying, remove the pan from the air fryer and spray the bread sticks with cooking spray. Flip sides and spray the other side too.
5. Place the pan back in the air fryer and fry for about 4 minutes or until golden brown.
6. Remove from the air fryer. Serve hot with maple syrup.

Breakfast Frittata

Ingredients:

- 8 cherry tomatoes, halved
- 6 eggs
- 2 tablespoons olive oil
- 2 tablespoons parmesan cheese, shredded
- 1 Italian sausage
- Salt to taste
- Pepper powder to taste

Method:

1. Preheat your air fryer to 180 degree C.
2. Add tomatoes and sausage to the baking accessory or baking dish. Place the baking dish in the air fryer and bake for 5 minutes.
3. Meanwhile add eggs, salt, pepper, oil and cheese to a bowl and whisk well.
4. Remove the baking dish and pour the egg mixture all over. Spread it evenly.
5. Place the baking dish back in the air fryer and bake for 5 minutes at 180 degree C.
6. Slice into wedges and serve.

Breakfast Soufflé

Ingredients:

- 4 eggs, beaten
- 1 small red bell pepper, finely chopped
- 2 tablespoons fresh parsley, finely chopped
- 4 tablespoons light cream
- Salt to taste
- Pepper powder to taste

Method:

1. Mix together all the ingredients in a bowl. Whisk well.
2. Pour in small heatproof custard cups or ramekins. Do not fill more than half the cups.
3. Place the cups in the air fryer basket and place the basket in the air fryer.
4. Air fry in a preheated air fryer at 200 degree C for 8 minutes. When done, remove from the basket.
5. If you like softer soufflés, then air fry for 5 minutes.
6. Serve hot.

English Breakfast

Ingredients:

- 2 eggs
- 4 medium sausages
- 1/2 a can baked beans
- 4 rashers un-smoked back bacon
- 4 slice multigrain bread, toasted

Method:

1. Place sausages and bacon in your preheated air fryer. Air fry for 10 minutes at 160 degree C.
2. Empty the baked beans into a ramekin. Crack the eggs into 2 other ramekins.
3. Place the ramekins in the air fryer along with the sausages and air fry for 10 minutes at 200 degree C.
4. Remove from the air fryer and invert on a serving platter.
5. Serve immediately with toasted bread.

Baked Ham, Mushroom and Egg

Ingredients:

- 8 small button Mushrooms, quartered
- 8 cherry tomatoes, halved
- 6 slices honey shaved ham
- 2 eggs
- 1/2 cup cheddar cheese
- 1 sprig rosemary, chopped (optional)
- Salt to taste
- Pepper powder to taste
- Salad greens to serve
- A little butter, melted - for greasing
- 2 whole wheat croissants

Method:

1. Grease the baking accessory or a baking dish, which is smaller than the air fryer with melted butter.
2. Layer the ingredients in any way you like and finally topped with cheese. You can put in a layer of cheese in the middle as well.
3. Make 2 small wells (cavities) in the ham layer. Crack an egg into each of the wells.
4. Season with salt and pepper. Sprinkle rosemary all over.
5. Place the baking dish on the basket of the air fryer. Place the croissants in the baking dish as well.
6. Bake in a preheated air fryer at 160 degree C for 8 minutes.
7. After 4 minutes, remove the croissants. You can remove it earlier if you like it less toasted.

8. You can adjust the timing according to the way you like your eggs to be cooked. Set lesser time if you like the eggs runny or slightly more time for half cooked eggs or more time for well cooked eggs.

9. To serve: Place the croissant on a serving plate. Place the baked ham and eggs over it. Place salad greens alongside and serve.

Breakfast Sandwiches

Ingredients:

- 2 whole wheat English muffins
- 2 eggs
- Salt to taste
- Pepper powder to taste
- 2 English bacons

Method:

1. Crack an egg each into ramekins or ovenproof cups. Season with salt and pepper.
2. Place the ramekins in a preheated air fryer.
3. Place the bacon and muffins alongside.
4. Air fry at 200 degree C for 6 minutes.
5. Remove the muffins from the air fryer after about a couple of minutes (toast it as per your desire)
6. Split the muffins.
7. When the bacon and eggs are done, place it in between the split muffin and make sandwiches.
8. Serve immediately.

Crispy Avocado Fries

Ingredients:

- 2 eggs, beaten
- 2 large avocadoes, peeled, pitted, cut into 8 slices each
- 1 cup whole wheat bread crumbs
- 1/2 cup whole wheat flour
- Juice of 1/2 lemon
- Salt to taste
- 1/2 teaspoon cayenne pepper
- 1/4 teaspoon pepper powder
- Greek yogurt to serve
- Honey to serve (optional)

Method:

1. Add flour to a bowl and add salt, pepper, and cayenne pepper to it.
2. Place panko bread crumbs in another bowl.
3. First dredge avocado slices in the flour mixture. Next dip it in the egg mixture and finally dredge it in the breadcrumbs. Now place it in the air fryer basket.
4. Place the air fryer basket in a preheated air fryer and air fry at 200 degree C for 6 minutes or until they are golden brown.
5. Transfer avocadoes on a serving platter.
6. Sprinkle lemon juice over it and serve with Greek yogurt. You can drizzle honey if you desire.

Avocado And Blueberry Muffins

Ingredients:

- 2 eggs
- 2 cups almond flour
- 1 cup blueberries, fresh or frozen
- 1/2 teaspoon baking soda
- 1 teaspoon baking powder
- 1/8 teaspoon salt
- 2 ripe avocadoes, peeled, pitted, mashed
- 2/3 cup caster sugar
- 1 cup plain Greek yogurt
- 1 teaspoon vanilla extract
  For streusel topping:
- 4 tablespoons almond flour
- 4 tablespoons butter, softened
- 4 tablespoons caster sugar

Method:

1. To make streusel topping: Mix together butter, flour and caster sugar to form a crumbly mixture. Place in the freezer for a while.
2. Meanwhile, make the muffins as follows:
3. Sift together flour, baking powder, baking soda and salt and set aside.
4. Add avocadoes and sugar to a bowl and mix well.
5. Add egg, one at a time and continue beating. Add vanilla extract and yogurt and beat again.
6. Add flour mixture a little at a time and mix well.
7. Add blueberries and fold.

8. Grease muffin cups and pour batter into it (half fill it). Divide and sprinkle streusel topping mixture over it.

9. Place the muffin cups in the air fryer basket and bake in a preheated air fryer at 180 degree C for 10 minutes or until the top is golden brown. A toothpick when inserted in the center should come out clean.

10. Remove the muffin cups from the air fryer and cool. Run a knife around the edges of the muffins and remove the muffins. Cool completely and serve.

Banana Bread / Banana muffins

Ingredients:

- 1 egg
- 3/4 cup whole wheat flour
- 2 1/2 tablespoons melted butter or olive oil
- 1/8 teaspoon baking soda
- 1/8 teaspoon ground cinnamon
- 2 tablespoons soft light brown sugar
- 1/4 cup sugar
- 1/2 teaspoon vanilla extract
- 2-4 tablespoons rolled oats for topping
- 1/8 teaspoon salt
- 2 tablespoons milk
- 1 medium very ripe banana, mashed

Method:

1. Preheat the air fryer to 180 degree C.
2. For dry ingredients: Sift flour, baking soda, salt, and cinnamon in a large bowl and set it aside.
3. For wet ingredients: Add egg, milk, banana, butter, and sugar, light brown sugar and vanilla to a bowl and whisk well. Add banana and stir well.
4. Pour the wet ingredients into the dry ingredients and mix well.
5. To make banana bread: Grease a small loaf tin (that fits well inside the air fryer basket) with a little melted butter. Pour the prepared batter into the loaf. Spread evenly.
6. Sprinkle oats all over the top of the batter.

7. Place the loaf tin inside the air fryer basket and bake at 180 degree C for about 15 -20 minutes or until done. A toothpick when inserted in the center should come out clean.

8. To make muffins: Pour the batter in greased muffin tins (half fill the muffin tins). Sprinkle oats on top and place in the air fryer basket. Bake at 180 degree C for about 15 minutes.

9. When done, remove from air fryer and cool for a while. Remove the loaf or muffins from the tin and place on a wire rack to cool completely.

Savory Toast

Ingredients:

- 1/2 cup chickpea flour
- 1 green chili, thinly sliced
- Water as required
- 1 tablespoon fresh cilantro, chopped
- 1 medium onion, finely chopped
- 1/2 teaspoon salt or to taste
- 1/4 teaspoon chili powder
- 6 slices whole wheat bread
- A little oil to brush

Method:

1. Add chickpea flour to a wide bowl. Add about 1/4-cup water and mix to get a batter of easily dropping consistency. Add more water if required, 1 tablespoon at a time and mix well each time.
2. Add rest of the ingredients except bread and mix well.
3. Place an aluminum foil on the bottom of the air fryer basket.
4. Apply the prepared batter on both the sides of the bread or dip it in the batter and immediately place on the air fryer basket.
5. Cook in batches.
6. Brush the batter coated bread slices with a little oil or you can use cooking spray too.
7. Air fry in a preheated air fryer at 200 degree C for 3 - 4 minutes or until done.
8. Serve with ketchup or a dip of your choice.

Baked Mini Quiches

Ingredients:

- 2 eggs
- 1 large onion, chopped
- 1 3/4 cups whole wheat flour
- 1/4 cup milk
- 3/4 cup butter
- 2 tablespoons oil
- Salt to taste
- Pepper powder to taste
- ¾ cup cottage cheese
- 1 ½ cup spinach, chopped

Method:

1. Preheat the air fryer.
2. Add flour, salt, butter, milk to a bowl and knead into a smooth dough. Refrigerate for about 15 minutes.
3. Meanwhile, place a skillet over medium heat. Add oil. When oil is heated, add onions and sauté until translucent.
4. Add spinach and sauté until spinach wilts. Remove from heat. Drain excess moisture from the spinach. You can squeeze out the excess moisture with your hands.
5. Whisk together eggs in a bowl and add cheese and spinach and mix well.
6. Remove the dough from the refrigerator and divide into 8 equal parts.

7. Roll the dough into a round, which is big enough to fit the bottom of the quiche mold.
8. Place the rolled dough in the molds. Place spinach filling over the dough.
9. Place the spinach filling over the dough.
10. Place the quiche molds inside the basket of the air fryer and place the basket inside the air fryer.
11. Air fry at 180 degree C for about 15 minutes.
12. Remove from the air fryer. Remove the quiche from the molds.
13. Serve warm or cold.

Chapter 6: Air Fryer Lunch Recipes

Cheese on toast

Ingredients:

- 4 tablespoons Branston pickle
- 4 slices whole wheat bread or multigrain bread, lightly toasted
- 4 tablespoons butter
- 4 tablespoons parmesan, shredded

Method:

1. Spread 1-tablespoon butter over each of the bread slices.
2. Spread a tablespoon of Branston pickle over the butter layer.
3. Sprinkle a tablespoon of cheese over each of the bread slices.
4. Place an aluminum foil sheet at the bottom of the air fryer basket.
5. Place the bread slices in the air fryer basket in a preheated air fryer at 200 degree C for 4 to 5 minutes.
6. Serve hot.

Crispy Baby corn Fritters

Ingredients:

- 2 cups chickpea flour (garbanzo flour)
- 1 pound baby corns, parboiled
- 1 teaspoon carom seeds
- 2 teaspoons garlic paste
- 2 teaspoons ginger paste
- 1 teaspoon salt or to taste
- 1/4 teaspoon chili powder
- A pinch baking soda
- 2 tablespoons fresh cilantro
- 1 1/2 cups water or more if required
- Cooking spray (optional)

Method:

1. Add chickpea flour to a wide bowl. Add about 1 1/2 cups water and mix to get a batter slightly thick but of dropping consistency. Add more water if required, 1 tablespoon at a time and mix well each time.
2. Add rest of the ingredients except baby corn and mix well.
3. Place an aluminum foil at the bottom of the air fryer basket.
4. Dip baby corn in the batter and immediately place on the air fryer basket. Spray with cooking spray.
5. Cook in batches. Place the air fryer basket in the air fryer.
6. Air fry in a preheated air fryer at 200 degree C for 3 - 4 minutes or until done.

7. Serve with ketchup or a dip of your choice.

Bell Pepper Oatmeal

Ingredients:

- 2 large bell peppers, halved lengthwise, deseeded
- 2 tablespoons cooked kidney beans
- 2 tablespoons cooked chick peas
- 2 cups oatmeal, cooked
- 1 teaspoon ground cumin
- 1/2 teaspoon paprika
- 1/2 teaspoon salt or to taste
- 1/4 teaspoon black pepper powder
- 1/4 cup yogurt

Method:

1. Place the bell peppers with its cut side down in the air fryer.
2. Air fry in a preheated air fryer at 180 degree C for 2-3 minutes. Remove from the air fryer and keep it aside.
3. Mix together rest of the ingredients in a bowl.
4. When the bell peppers are cool enough to handle, divide and stuff this mixture into the bell peppers.
5. Place it back in the air fryer and air fry at 180 degree C for 4 minutes.
6. Serve hot.

Chili Garlic Potato Wedges

Ingredients:

- 4 large potatoes, chopped into wedges
- 1 teaspoon ground cumin
- 1/2 teaspoon turmeric powder
- 1 teaspoon red chili flakes
- 2 teaspoons garlic paste
- 1 teaspoon dry mango powder
- 1 teaspoon salt or to taste
- Cooking spray

Method:

1. Mix together all the ingredients except potatoes in a small bowl. Rub this mixture over the potatoes. Let the potatoes marinate for at least 30-45 minutes.
2. Place the potato wedges in a preheated air fryer. Spray with cooking spray and air fry at 180 degree C for 12-15 minutes or until done. Turn the wedges around a couple of times in between.
3. Serve hot with a salad of your choice.

Spinach n Cheese Lasagna

Ingredients:

- 1 large onion, chopped
- 3 whole wheat dry lasagna sheets
- 1/2 cup parmesan cheese, shredded
- 1/2 cup ricotta cheese, shredded
- 3 cups spinach, frozen, thawed, squeezed of excess moisture
- 1 tablespoon butter
- 1 cup pesto sauce of your choice
- Salt to taste
- Pepper powder to taste
- 1-2 tablespoons Italian seasoning

Method:

1. Grease the baking accessory or baking dish, which is smaller than the air fryer with butter.
2. Place a lasagna sheet at the bottom of the baking accessory.
3. Next layer with 1/3 the spinach followed by 1/3 the onions, 1/3 the pesto sauce, salt, pepper, and 1/3 the ricotta cheese.
4. Repeat step 2,3 twice more.
5. In the last layer, sprinkle Parmesan cheese on top. Cover the baking dish with a foil.
6. Place the baking accessory inside the air fryer basket.
7. Air fry in a preheated air fryer at 180 degree C for about 25-30 minutes. Uncover and continue cooking for 3-4 minutes.

8. Remove from air fryer and cool for 5 minutes before serving.

Quinoa stuffed Mushrooms

Ingredients:

- 1/2 cup quinoa, rinsed, cook according to instructions on the package
- 2 tablespoons walnuts, chopped into small pieces
- 8 large mushrooms, remove the stems
- 4 button mushrooms, finely chopped
- 1/2 teaspoon chili powder or to taste
- Salt to taste
- Pepper powder to taste
- 4 tablespoons parmesan cheese, shredded

Method:

1. Mix together in a bowl, cooked quinoa, chopped mushrooms, walnuts, chili powder, salt, pepper and cheese.
2. Stuff this filling in the large mushrooms.
3. Place the mushrooms in a preheated air fryer. Air fry at 190 degree C for 7 minutes or until done.

Chicken Drumsticks

Ingredients:

- 2 tablespoons honey or brown sugar
- 8 chicken drumsticks, boneless
- 1/2 teaspoon black pepper powder
- 1/2 teaspoon salt or to taste
- 1/2 cup Dijon mustard
- 4 tablespoons olive oil
- 2 tablespoons mixed herbs

Method:

1. Mix together all the ingredients in a large bowl. Toss well, cover and refrigerate for at least 5-6 hours. Toss the ingredients in between a couple of times.
2. Remove from the refrigerator and preheat an air fryer to 160 degree C
3. Place an aluminum foil inside the air fryer basket. Place the chicken drumsticks inside the air fryer basket.
4. Air fry at 160 degree C for about 12 minutes or until done.

Baked Butter Crayfish

Ingredients:

- 6 crayfish, rinsed, scrubbed
- 6-7 small cubes butter
- 6-7 small cream cubes
- 2 teaspoons garlic powder
- 1/4 teaspoon salt or to taste
- 1/4 teaspoon pepper powder
- 1/4 teaspoon red chili flakes
- Whole wheat spaghetti, cooked, to serve (optional)

Method:

1. Place an aluminum foil at the bottom of the air fryer basket. Place the crayfish with its bottom side up.
2. Place butter and cream cubes all over the fish.
3. Sprinkle salt, pepper, garlic powder, and chili flakes all over the fish.
4. Now seal the crayfish with foil. Place the sealed crayfish packet in the air fryer basket.
5. Air fry in a preheated air fryer at 190 degree C for 18-20 minutes.
6. When done serve with spaghetti and a spaghetti sauce of your choice.

Mushrooms with Chicken sausage

Ingredients:

- 10 small Portobello mushrooms, washed, stems removed
- 1/2 cup mozzarella cheese
- 2 cups chicken sausages, chopped into small pieces
- 2-3 tablespoons mayonnaise

Method:

1. Mix together in a bowl sausages and mayonnaise.
2. Place an aluminum foil at the bottom of the air fryer basket.
3. Place mushrooms over the foil. Spread the sausage mixture over the mushrooms.
4. Sprinkle cheese all over.
5. Air fry in a preheated air fryer at 1820 degree C for 5 minutes or until the cheese is light brown.

Tandoori Chicken Drummettes

Ingredients:

- 1 dozen chicken drummettes, make a few slits with a sharp knife
- 2 cloves garlic, peeled
- 1 inch piece ginger, peeled, chopped
- 3/4 cup low fat yogurt
- 1/2 teaspoon chili powder
- 1 green chilies
- 1/2 teaspoon salt or to taste
- Sliced onions to serve
- 1 teaspoon garam masala (Indian spice blend)
- A few drops orange food coloring (optional)
- Juice of a lemon
- A few lemon wedges to serve
- Cooking spray

Method:

1. Blend together in a blender, ginger, garlic, chili powder, green chili, yogurt, and garam masala to a smooth paste and set aside.
2. Mix together in a small bowl, lemon juice, salt and food coloring. Rub this over the chicken drummettes. Refrigerate for about 30 minutes.
3. Remove from the refrigerator and add the blended mixture over it, toss well.
4. Cover and refrigerate for 6-7 hours. Stir in between a few times.
5. Remove from the refrigerator an hour before cooking.

6. Place the chicken drummettes on the air fryer grill pan. Retain the marinade.
7. Air fry the drummettes in a preheated air fryer at 200 degree C for 10 minutes.
8. Brush the drummettes with the marinade. Spray a little cooking spray.
9. Air fry for another 3-4 minutes.
10. Serve with sliced onions and lemon wedges.

Rosemary Chicken

Ingredients:

- 1 chicken breast, halved, rinsed, pat dried
- 2 teaspoons honey
- 2 sprigs rosemary, roughly chopped
- 1 teaspoon chili flakes
- Freshly ground black pepper
- Salt to taste
- 1 teaspoon olive oil

Method:

1. Spread oil over the chicken pieces. Sprinkle salt, pepper, chili flakes, rosemary and honey over it. Set aside for a while to marinate.
2. Place the chicken in the air fryer basket and place the basket in the air fryer.
3. Air fry in a preheated air fryer at 180 degree C for 12-15 minutes or until cooked.
4. Serve with sweet potato fries and a salad of your choice.

Chicken Wings

Ingredients:

- 8 chicken wings, thawed
- 1/2 teaspoon hot paprika
- 2 cloves garlic, minced
- 1 teaspoon ground ginger
- 1/2 teaspoon ground cumin
- 1/2 teaspoon freshly ground black pepper
- ¼ teaspoon sweet chili sauce
- 1/4 teaspoon salt or to taste
- Cooking spray

Method:

1. Mix together garlic, ginger, pepper, paprika, cumin and salt in a bowl. Rub the chicken wings with this mixture.
2. Place the chicken wings in the air fryer basket. Spray with cooking spray. Place the basket in the air fryer.
3. Air fry in a preheated air fryer at 180 degree C for 15 minutes. Flip the chicken wings once in between. Spray with cooking spray.
4. Serve hot with sweet chili sauce.

Ratatouille

Ingredients:

- 1 yellow bell pepper, deseeded, chopped into 2 cm cubes
- 1 red bell pepper, deseeded, chopped into 2 cm cubes
- 1 tomato, deseeded chopped into 2 cm cubes
- 1 courgette, chopped into 2 cm cubes
- 1 large onion, chopped into 2 cm cubes
- 1 aubergine, chopped into 2 cm cubes
- 1/2 tablespoon olive oil
- 1 clove garlic, crushed
- 1 teaspoon dried Provencal herbs
- Freshly ground black pepper
- Salt to taste

Method:

1. Mix together courgette, aubergine, bell peppers, tomatoes, and onions in a baking dish.
2. Add garlic, oil, herbs, salt and pepper.
3. Place the baking dish in the air fryer basket and place the basket in the air fryer.
4. Air fry in a preheated air fryer at 200 degree C for 15 minutes. Stir the vegetables in between a couple of times.
5. Serve hot with air fried chicken or cutlets.

French Fries

Ingredients:

- 2 large potatoes, peeled, chopped into fries
- Salt to taste
- Pepper powder to taste
- Piri piri powder to taste
- 1 teaspoon oil

Method:

1. Place the potatoes in a bowl of cold water for 30 minutes. Drain and pat dry with a kitchen towel.
2. Place the fries in a bowl and drizzle oil over it. Toss well.
3. Place the potatoes in the air fryer basket. Air fry in a preheated air fryer at 185 degree C for 25 minutes.
4. Remove from the fryer and season with piri piri, salt and pepper.
5. Serve hot.

Mushroom Cream

Ingredients:

- 1 dozen mushrooms, chopped
- 1/2 cup cheese of your choice, grated + extra to top
- 1 piece bacon, chopped
- 2 tablespoons carrots, chopped
- 2 tablespoons onions, chopped
- 2 tablespoons green bell pepper, chopped
- 1/4 cup sour cream

Method:

1. Place a pan over medium heat. Add all the ingredients except cream and cream cheese and sauté for a few minutes until vegetables are soft.
2. Transfer into the air fryer baking accessory. Add cream and cheese and mix.
3. Sprinkle extra cheese on top.
4. Place the baking dish in the air fryer basket and place the basket in the air fryer.
5. Air fry in a preheated air fryer at 180 degree C for 10 minutes.

Crumbed Fish

Ingredients:

- 6 pieces fish fillets
- 2 tablespoons vegetable oil
- Salt to taste
- Pepper powder to taste
- 1/4 cup whole wheat bread crumbs
- Lemon wedges to serve

Method:

1. Mix together in a bow, breadcrumbs, oil, salt, and pepper.
2. Dredge the fillets in the breadcrumbs mixture and place in the air fryer basket.
3. Place the baking dish in the air fryer basket and place the basket in the air fryer.
4. Air fry in a preheated air fryer at 180 degree C for 12 minutes or until done.
5. Serve with a salad of your choice

Chapter 7: Air Fryer Dinner Recipes

Appetizer Recipes

Potato n Cheese Balls

Ingredients:

- 4 medium potatoes, boiled, peeled, mashed
- 1/2 cup mozzarella cheese cubes (cut into small cubes of about 1 cm)
- 2 slices whole wheat bread
- 1/2 teaspoon black pepper powder
- 1/2 teaspoon chili powder or to taste
- 1/2 teaspoon cumin powder
- 1/2 teaspoon salt or to taste
- 2 tablespoons cornstarch to dust

Method:

1. Take some water in a bowl. Dip the slices of bread in it and take it out immediately. Place between your hands and press out as much of water as possible. Add this to mashed potatoes.
2. Add rest of the ingredients except cheese and cornstarch and mix well.
3. Divide the mixture into 6-7 equal portions.
4. Place a piece of cheese in the center of the mixture and shape into balls.
5. Lightly dredge the balls in cornstarch and place in the air fryer basket.

6. Air fry in a preheated air fryer at 200 degree C for 10 minutes or until golden brown.

Vegetable Fritters

Ingredients:

- 1 small head cauliflower, chopped into small pieces of about 1 cm each
- 1 large onion, chopped
- 1 large potato, peeled, chopped into small pieces of about 1 cm each
- 1 cup spinach, rinsed, chopped
- 1 green chili, chopped
- 1/4 teaspoon chili powder
- 1 cup garbanzo flour or chickpea flour
- 1 teaspoon ground cumin
- 1 teaspoon garlic paste or garlic powder
- 1 teaspoon salt or to taste
- Cooking spray

Method:

1. Mix together all the ingredients except chickpea flour and set aside for a while. Some amount of water is released from the vegetables.
2. Add chickpea flour and mix well. Add a couple of tablespoons of water or more if required and mix well. You should get a mixture which should be thick but of dropping consistency.
3. Place an aluminum foil or butter paper in the air fryer basket and drop fritters over it. Spray with cooking spray.
4. Place the air fryer basket in a preheated air fryer.
5. Air fry at 200 degree C for about 10 minutes or until done.

6. Serve with ketchup or mint chutney.

Potato Croquettes

Ingredients:

- 1 large potato, boiled, peeled, mashed
- 2 tablespoons parmesan cheese, grated
- A pinch ground nutmeg
- 1 tablespoon flour
- 1 tablespoon fresh chives, chopped
- 1/4 teaspoon salt or to taste
- 1/8 teaspoon pepper powder or to taste
  For coating:
- 1/4 cup whole grain breadcrumbs
- 1 tablespoon vegetable oil

Method:

1. Mix together all the ingredients of the croquettes until well combined.
2. Divide the mixture and shape into balls or desired shape.
3. Mix together oil and breadcrumbs until crumbly.
4. Roll the balls in the breadcrumbs and place in the air fryer basket.
5. Place the basket in the air fryer.
6. Air fry in a preheated air fryer at 200 degree C for 8 minutes or until golden brown.
7. Serve with ketchup or dip of your choice.

Ricotta Balls

Ingredients:

- 2 cups ricotta, grated
- 2 eggs, separated
- 2 tablespoons chives, finely chopped
- 2 tablespoons fresh basil, finely chopped
- 4 tablespoons whole wheat flour
- 1/4 teaspoon salt or to taste
- 1/4 teaspoon pepper powder or to taste
- 1 teaspoon orange zest, grated
  For coating:
- 1/4 cup whole wheat breadcrumbs
- 1 tablespoon vegetable oil

Method:

1. Mix together in a bowl, yolks, flour, salt, pepper, chives and zest. Add ricotta and mix well with your hands.
2. Divide the mixture and shape into balls or desired shape.
3. Mix together oil and breadcrumbs until crumbly.
4. Roll the balls in the breadcrumbs and place in the air fryer basket.
5. Place the basket in the air fryer.
6. Air fry in a preheated air fryer at 200 degree C for 8 minutes or until golden brown.
7. Serve with ketchup or dip of your choice.

Mini Empanadas

Ingredients:

- 1 pound pizza dough
- 1 cup chorizo, chopped into small cubes
- 4 tablespoons parsley, minced
- 2 shallots, minced
- 1 small red bell pepper, chopped into very small pieces

Method:

1. Place a skillet over medium low heat. Add chorizo, shallot, and bell pepper and sauté until bell peppers are soft.
2. Remove from heat and add parsley. Let the mixture cool completely.
3. Roll the dough and cut small rounds of about 5-6 cm diameter.
4. Place about a spoonful of the mixture on one half of the round. Fold the other half over it (to form a semi circle). Press the edges so as to fasten.
5. Place the empanadas in batches in the air fryer basket.
6. Place the basket in a preheated air fryer and air fry at 200 degree C for about 10 minutes or until golden brown.
7. Serve lukewarm.

Crispy Fried Spring Rolls

Ingredients:

- 4 - 5 spring roll wrappers
- 1 cup cooked chicken breast, shredded
- 1 cup mushrooms, chopped into small pieces
- 1 egg beaten
- 1 green onion, thinly sliced
- 1 carrot, finely chopped
- 1 green bell pepper, finely chopped
- 1 onion, finely chopped
- 8-10 green beans, thinly sliced
- 1 inch piece ginger, minced
- 2 cloves garlic, minced
- 1 teaspoon cornstarch
- 1/4 teaspoon white pepper powder
- 1/4 teaspoon salt or to taste
- 2 teaspoons soy sauce
- 1 teaspoon hot sauce
- 2 teaspoons vegetable oil + extra for brushing

Method:

1. Place a skillet over medium high heat. Add oil. When oil is heated, add onions and sauté until onions are translucent.
2. Increase the heat to high. Add ginger, garlic, carrots, mushrooms, beans, pepper, and green onions and sauté for a couple of minutes.
3. Add soy sauce, hot sauce and salt and sauté until the liquid dries up.
4. Remove from heat and cool.

65

5. Mix together egg and cornstarch in a small bowl.
6. Place the spring roll wrappers on your work area.
7. Divide and place the filling in the middle of the wrappers, all over the wrapper. Roll. Seal the edges with the egg paste.
8. Brush the rolls with a little oil and place in the air fryer basket. Fry in batches.
9. Place the air fryer basket in a preheated air fryer.
10. Air fry at 200 degree C for 4-5 minutes or until golden brown and crisp.
11. Remove from the air fryer and place on a plate. Using a sharp knife cut the roll into 3-4 pieces.
12. Serve with hot sauce or sweet chili sauce.

Cheesy Mushrooms

Ingredients:

- 1 pound button mushrooms, rinsed, pat dried
- 1/2 cup parmesan cheese, finely grated
- 1 large egg, whisked well
- 2 tablespoons whole wheat flour
- 1/2 cup whole wheat bread crumbs
- Salt to taste
- Pepper powder to taste

Method:

1. Mix together breadcrumbs and cheese in a bowl.
2. Place flour in a plate.
3. First dredge mushrooms in flour. Next dip in egg and finally dredge in breadcrumbs mixture. Place mushrooms in the air fryer basket.
4. Place the air fryer basket in a preheated air fryer.
5. Air fry at 180 degree C for 7 minutes or until golden brown. Turn the mushrooms around a couple of times.
6. Remove from the air fryer and place on a serving platter. Serve with a dip of your choice.

Fish Fry

Ingredients:

- 1/2 cup whole wheat bread crumbs
- 3 fish fillets preferably catfish, halved
- Juice of 1 1/2 lemons
- Zest of 1 1/2 lemons, grated
- 1 large egg, whisked
- Salt to taste
- Pepper powder to taste
- 2 tablespoons parsley
- 1 cup tortilla chips

Method:

1. Sprinkle lemon juice over the fish fillets and set aside.
2. Add breadcrumbs, zest, parsley, tortillas, salt and pepper to a food processor and pulse until well combined.
3. Remove and place a slightly deep dish.
4. First dip fish fillets in egg and dredge in the bread crumbs mixture and place in the air fryer basket.
5. Place the air fryer basket in the air fryer.
6. Air fry at 180 degree C for 15 minutes or until golden brown. Turn the fillets around a couple of times.
7. Remove from the air fryer and place on a serving platter. Serve with a dip of your choice.

Stuffed Mushrooms with Sour Cream

Ingredients:

- 1 dozen medium sized mushrooms (remove stem and chop the stems finely and set aside)
- 1 rasher bacon
- 1 small carrot, peeled, finely chopped
- 1 small onion, finely chopped
- 2 tablespoons green bell pepper, finely chopped
- 1/4 cup sour cream
- 1/2 cup parmesan cheese + extra for sprinkling

Method:

1. Place a skillet over medium heat. Add bacon, onion, bell pepper, carrots, and chopped mushroom stem and sauté until vegetables are soft.
2. Add sour cream and cheese and cook until cheese melts.
3. Fill this mixture in the mushrooms and place mushrooms in the air fryer basket. Sprinkle cheese over the mushrooms.
4. Place the air fryer basket in the air fryer.
5. Air fry at 180 degree C for 8 minutes.
6. Remove from the air fryer and place on a serving platter. Serve with a dip of your choice.

Garlic Mushrooms

Ingredients:

- 2 dozen mushrooms, remove stems
- 4 teaspoons olive oil
- 2 slices whole wheat bread made into crumbs
- 2 tablespoons flat leaf parsley, finely chopped
- 4 cloves garlic, minced
- Freshly ground black pepper to taste
- Salt to taste

Method:

1. Mix together in a bowl, breadcrumbs, garlic, salt, pepper, and parsley.
2. Add olive oil and mix to get a crumble mixture.
3. Stuff this mixture in the mushroom caps and place in the air fryer basket.
4. Place the air fryer basket in the air fryer.
5. Air fry at 180 degree C for 8 minutes.
6. Remove from the air fryer and place on a serving platter. Serve with a dip of your choice.

Main Course Recipes

Pork Tenderloin

Ingredients:

- 2 pork tenderloins of about 300 grams each
- 2 tablespoons olive oil
- 2 onions, thinly sliced
- 1 red bell pepper, thinly sliced
- 1 yellow bell pepper, thinly sliced
- 1 tablespoon mustard
- 1 1/2 tablespoons Provencal herbs
- Salt to taste
- Freshly ground black pepper to taste

Method:

1. Add bell peppers, onions, herbs, salt and pepper to the baking accessory or a small baking dish that fits well into the air fryer. Mix.
2. Add about a tablespoon of oil to it.
3. Mix together in a bowl, mustard, salt and pepper. Rub this mixture over the pork. Brush the pieces with remaining oil.
4. Place the pork pieces over the bell pepper mixture. Place the dish in the air fryer basket.
5. Place the air fryer basket in the air fryer.
6. Air fry at 200 degree C for 15 minutes. After about 7 - 8 minutes stir the peppers and tenderloin as well.
7. Remove from the air fryer and place on a serving platter.

Pork Satay with Peanut Sauce

Ingredients:

- ¾ cup lean pork chops, chopped into 1/3 inch cubes
- 2 cloves garlic, crushed
- 1 teaspoon chili paste or chili sauce
- 1 inch piece fresh ginger, grated
- 1 small onion, finely chopped
- 2 tablespoons sweet soy sauce
- 1/2 cup coconut milk
- 1 tablespoon vegetable oil
- 1/2 teaspoon ground coriander
- ¼ cup roasted peanuts, unsalted, ground

Method:

1. Mix together in a bowl, a clove garlic, ginger, 1/2 teaspoon chili paste, 1/2 the soy sauce and 1/2 the oil.
2. Add pork chops to the bowl and mix well. Let it marinate in the mixture for at least 30 minutes,
3. Place the marinated pork pieces in the air fryer basket and place the basket in the air fryer.
4. Air fry in a preheated air fryer at 200 degree C for 12 minutes or until brown. Turn the chops around once half way through.
5. Serve hot.
6. Meanwhile make the peanut sauce as follows: Place a small skillet over medium heat. Add remaining oil. When oil is heated, add onion and 1 clove garlic and sauté until onion is translucent.

7. Add coriander and sauté for a few seconds until fragrant.
8. Add coconut milk, peanuts, remaining chili paste, and remaining soy sauce. Mix well and bring to a boil. Lower heat and simmer for 5 minutes, if the sauce is too thick, then add a little water to dilute. Taste and adjust the seasoning if necessary. You can add more soy sauce or chili paste.
9. Serve pork with peanut sauce.

Crispy Roast Pork

Ingredients:

- 3 pounds pork belly, pluck off excess hair if any, well cooked in a pot of water
  For dry rub:
- 1 teaspoon 5 spice powder
- 1/2 teaspoon white pepper powder
- 1 teaspoon garlic salt or 1/2 teaspoon garlic powder + 1/2 teaspoon salt
  To rub over skin:
- 1/4 cup lemon juice
- 1/2 teaspoon salt

Method:

1. Pat dry the cooked pork and air dry until it is completely dried. Pierce the skin of the pork with a sharp skewer. Loosen the skin lightly with a knife.
2. Mix together all the ingredients of the rub. Rub this mixture all over the meat of the pork.
3. Mix together lemon juice and salt and rub all over the skin.
4. Place an aluminum foil at the bottom of the air fryer basket.
5. Place the pork pieces with its skin facing upwards in the basket.
6. Place the air fryer basket in the air fryer.
7. Air fry at 160 degree C for 30 minute.
8. Remove from the air fryer and serve.

Roast Beef

Ingredients:

- 2 pounds rump roast
- Freshly ground black pepper
- 1/2 teaspoon salt
- 2 tablespoons BBQ sauce
- 5-6 potatoes, chopped into bite sized pieces.
- 1 tablespoon olive oil

Method:

1. Mix together all the ingredients except beef and potatoes and rub this mixture all over the beef. Add potatoes and mix again. Set aside for a while to marinate.
2. Place an aluminum foil at the bottom of the air fryer basket.
3. Now remove the roast and place in the air fryer basket.
4. Place the air fryer basket in the air fryer.
5. Air fry in a preheated air fryer at 200 degree C for 30 minutes. After about 15 minutes, add the potatoes to the air fryer.
6. Remove from the air fryer and serve with a gravy or sauce of your choice.

Brazilian Meat Balls

Ingredients:

For meat balls:
- 2 eggs
- 2 pounds ground beef
- 1 onion, chopped
- 2 tablespoons garlic, minced
- 1/2 cup parsley, chopped
- 1 green bell pepper, chopped
- 1/2 cup spring onions, thinly chopped
- 2 fresh long red chilies, finely chopped
- 1 1/2 cups whole wheat flour
- 1 teaspoon salt or to taste
  For vinaigrette dressing:
- 1 small onion, minced
- 2 tablespoons yellow bell pepper, finely chopped
- 2 tablespoons red bell pepper, finely chopped
- 2 tablespoons green bell pepper, finely chopped
- 1 fresh long red chili, finely chopped
- 1/4 cup extra virgin olive oil
- 1/2 cup white vinegar
- 1 tablespoon piri piri powder
- 1/2 teaspoon salt or to taste

Method:

1. To make vinaigrette dressing: Mix together all the ingredients in a bowl and set aside.

2. To make meatballs: Mix together all the ingredients for the meatball. Divide the mixture and make balls of about 4 cm diameter using your hands.

3. Place balls in the air fryer basket. Do not crowd. Place only one layer. The rest can be cooked in batches.

4. Place the air fryer basket in a preheated air fryer.

5. Air fry at 160 degree C for 10 minutes.

6. Increase the temperature to 180 degree C and fry for 3-4 minutes more.

7. Serve the balls with vinaigrette.

Schnitzel Parmigiana

Ingredients:

- 2 pre-crumbed schnitzel, beef or chicken
- 1/2 cup parmesan cheese, grated
- 1/3 cup pasta sauce of your choice

Method:

1. Place the schnitzel in the air fryer basket.
2. Place the air fryer basket in the air fryer.
3. Air fry in a preheated air fryer at 180 degree C for 15 minutes. Remove from the air fryer and add pasta sauce over the schnitzel.
4. Sprinkle cheese all over it.
5. Air fry for another 5 minutes until the cheese melts.

Meat Stuffed Courgette

Ingredients:

- 2 large courgettes
- 2 cloves garlic, crushed
- 2 cups lean ground beef
- 1/2 cup feta cheese, crumbled
- 1 tablespoon mild paprika powder
- Freshly ground black pepper to taste
- Salt to taste

Method:

1. Slice off the ends of the courgettes. Slice each courgette into 6 equal parts.
2. Scoop out the flesh with a teaspoon leaving about 1 cm from the bottom and 1/2 centimeter from the sides.
3. Sprinkle salt inside the scooped courgettes.
4. Mix together rest of the ingredients in a bowl. Divide this mixture into 12 equal portions and stuff in the hollow courgette slices. Press well.
5. Cook the courgettes in batches.
6. Place a few courgette slices in the air fryer basket. Place the basket in the air fryer.
7. Air fry in a preheated air fryer at 180 degree C for 20 minutes.
8. Similarly fry the remaining courgette slices.
9. Serve hot with cherry tomatoes to complete a meal.

Meat Loaf

Ingredients:

- 3 1/2 cups lean ground beef
- 2 eggs, lightly beaten
- 1/2 cup salami or chorizo sausage, finely chopped
- 4 mushrooms, chopped into thick slices
- 2 tablespoons fresh thyme
- 1 medium onion, finely chopped
- 6 tablespoons whole wheat breadcrumbs
- 2 teaspoons freshly ground black pepper powder
- Salt to taste
- A little olive oil to brush

Method:

1. Mix together all the ingredients except mushrooms in a bowl. Knead to form a dough.
2. Divide the dough into 2 and place in 2 baking accessories or baking pans. Using a spatula spread the mixture well.
3. Divide the mushroom slices and place on top of the meat in both the pans. Press the mushrooms slightly into the meat.
4. Brush the top with olive oil.
5. Place one pan in the air fryer basket and place the basket in the air fryer.
6. Air fry in a preheated air fryer at 200 degree C for 25 minutes or until brown. Remove from the air fryer and let it stand for 10-12 minutes.
7. Place the next pan in the air fryer and repeat step 6.

8. Slice into wedges and serve with a salad of your choice.

Roast Potatoes with Tuna

Ingredients:

- 4 medium potatoes
- 1/2 a can of tuna in oil, drained
- 1 teaspoon olive oil
- 1 green onion, sliced
- 1/2 teaspoon chili powder
- 1 tablespoon Greek yogurt
- 1/2 tablespoon capers
- Freshly ground black pepper to taste
- Salt to taste

Method:

1. Soak the potatoes in water for about 30 minutes and pat dry with a kitchen towel.
2. Brush potatoes with olive oil.
3. Place the potatoes in the air fryer basket and air fry for 30 minutes in a preheated air fryer at 180 degree C.
4. Place tuna in a bowl. Add yogurt and chili powder. Mash well. Add half the green onions, salt and pepper to taste.
5. Slit the potatoes lengthwise a little. Slightly press the potatoes to open up a bit.
6. Stuff the tuna mixture into it. Place on a serving plate.
7. Sprinkle some chili powder and remaining green onions over the potatoes. Serve with capers and a salad of your choice.

Garlic Butter White Clams in Wine

Ingredients:

- 2-3 small cubes of salted butter (about 1 cm cubes),
- 1 pound clams
- 3-4 tablespoons rice wine
- 1 teaspoon ginger, peeled, minced
- 1 teaspoon garlic, minced
- Pepper powder to taste
- Salt to taste

Method:

1. Place an aluminum foil at the bottom of the air fryer basket. Place the clams with its bottom side up.
2. Place butter, ginger and garlic all over the clams.
3. Spread it all over the clams. Sprinkle salt and pepper over it.
4. Lift the foil from all sides and pour wine over it. Immediately seal the clams with foil. Wine should not leak from the packet. Place the sealed clam packet in the air fryer basket.
5. Air fry in a preheated air fryer at 200 degree C for about 14 - 15 minutes.
6. The clams should open up. Do not eat the unopened clams; discard it.

Gambas Pil Pil with Sweet potatoes

Ingredients:

- 3 large sweet potatoes, chop into slices
- 6 king size prawns, cleaned, deveined
- 2 stalks lemon grass
- 2 shallots, chopped
- 2 cloves garlic, finely sliced
- 1 red chili pepper, deseeded, finely sliced
- 3 tablespoons olive oil, divided
- 1/2 teaspoon smoked paprika powder
- 1 tablespoon fresh rosemary, finely chopped
- 1/2 tablespoon honey
- 1 lime, cut into wedges

Method:

1. Mix together in a large bowl, garlic, red chili pepper, garlic, onion, paprika, and 2 tablespoons olive oil.
2. Add prawns and toss well. Let it marinate for 2 - 3 hours.
3. Place sweet potatoes in a bowl. Add remaining oil, rosemary and honey.
4. Place the sweet potatoes in the air fryer basket and air fry for 15minutes in a preheated air fryer at 180 degree C.
5. Now fix the prawns on to the lemongrass stalks and place the prawns along with the lemongrass stalk in the air fryer.
6. Increase the temperature to 200 degree C and air fry for 5 minutes.

7. Serve sweet potatoes and prawns with lime wedges.

Prawn Cutlet

Ingredients:

- 1 cup prawns, minced
- 1 medium onion, finely chopped
- 1 cup whole grain breadcrumbs
- 1 tablespoon ginger paste
- 1 tablespoon garlic paste
- 1/2 teaspoon turmeric powder
- 1 teaspoon cumin powder
- 1 teaspoon chili powder
- 1 teaspoon dry mango powder
- 1 teaspoon salt or to taste
- A little wheat flour for dusting

Method:

1. Mix together all the ingredients in a bowl. Shape into cutlets. Dust with flour.
2. Place a few cutlets in the air fryer basket. Place the basket in the air fryer.
3. Air fry in a preheated air fryer at 180 degree C for 5 - 6 minutes.
4. Similarly fry the remaining cutlets in batches.
5. Serve hot with whole wheat bread slices.

Salmon Croquettes

Ingredients:

- 1/2 cup spring onions, sliced
- 1/2 cup celery, finely chopped
- 2 tins salmon, drained, flaked
- 10 tablespoons wheat germ
- 2 tablespoons fresh dill, chopped
- Cooking spray
- 1 teaspoon garlic granules
- 2 eggs

Method:

1. Mix together all the ingredients except wheat germ in a bowl.
2. Divide and shape into balls of about 2-inch diameter.
3. Dredge the balls in wheat germ.
4. Place the balls in the air fryer basket. Place the basket in the air fryer.
5. Air fry in a preheated air fryer at 180 degree C for 7-8 minutes or until golden brown.
6. Similarly fry the remaining balls in batches.
7. Serve hot with whole wheat bread slices.

Grilled Fish Fillets with Pesto Sauce

Ingredients:

- 4 cloves garlic
- 1/4 cup pine nuts
- 6 white fish fillets
- 1/4 cup fresh basil, chopped
- 2 tablespoons olive oil
- Salt to taste
- Pepper powder to taste
- 2 tablespoons parmesan cheese, grated
- ¼ teaspoon extra virgin olive oil

Method:

1. Brush fish fillets with a little oil. Sprinkle salt and pepper over the fillets.
2. Place the fish fillets in the air fryer basket and place the basket in the air fryer.
3. Air fry in a preheated air fryer at 200 degree C for 12 minutes or until brown.
4. To make pesto sauce: Blend together basil, garlic, pine nuts, oil, parmesan cheese, salt, pepper and olive oil until smooth.
5. Serve the fillets with pesto sauce.

Grilled Chicken

Ingredients:

- 6 chicken pieces, make a few slits with a sharp knife
- 1 cup plain Greek yogurt
- 1 teaspoon chili powder
- 1 teaspoon salt
- 1 teaspoon ground cumin
- 1 teaspoon ground coriander
- 1/2 teaspoon turmeric powder
- Lemon wedges to serve.
- Cooking spray

Method:

1. Mix together in a large bowl all the ingredients except lemon wedges,
2. Cover and refrigerate for 6-7 hours. Toss in between a couple of times.
3. Remove from the refrigerator about an hour before frying.
4. Place an aluminum foil in the air fryer basket. Place the chicken pieces in the basket and spray with cooking spray. Place the basket in the air fryer.
5. Air fry in a preheated air fryer at 200 degree C for 15 minutes or until brown. Turn the chicken pieces in between a couple of times.
6. Serve chicken with lemon wedges.

Chicken Fillets with Brie and Cured Ham

Ingredients:

- 6 slices cured ham, halved
- 3 large chicken fillets
- 2 tablespoons chives, finely chopped
- Freshly ground black pepper powder
- Salt to taste
- 6 small slices Brie cheese
- 1 tablespoon olive oil

Method:

1. Slit the chicken fillet pieces horizontally up to about 1 cm from the edges.
2. Sprinkle salt and pepper inside the fillet through the slits.
3. Stuff a slice of Brie cheese and chives inside the slit.
4. Wrap each stuffed chicken fillet with a slice of ham around it.
5. Brush with olive oil and place in the air fryer basket. Place the basket in the air fryer.
6. Air fry in a preheated air fryer at 180 degree C for 15 minutes or until brown. Turn the chicken pieces in between a couple of times.
7. Serve with mashed potatoes.

Chicken Tenderloins

Ingredients:

- 4 chicken tenderloins, skinless, boneless (boneless chicken breasts), cut into thin strips
- 2 teaspoons honey
- 1/4 cup Italian style salad dressing
- 2 teaspoons lime juice

Method:

1. Mix together all the ingredients except chicken in a small bowl.
2. Place chicken strips in the baking accessory. Pour the mixture over it.
3. Cover and place in the refrigerator for at least an hour.
4. Discard the marinade and place the baking accessory in the air fryer basket.
5. Air fry in a preheated air fryer at 180 degree C for 12 -15 minutes or until brown. Turn the chicken pieces in between a couple of times.

Chicken Mania

Ingredients:

- 1 egg, beaten
- 2 teaspoons melted butter or olive oil
- 4 pieces chicken tenderloins
- 1/4 cup whole wheat bread crumbs
- Salt to taste
- Pepper powder to taste

Method:

1. Mix together breadcrumbs and oil in a bowl.
2. Season chicken with salt and pepper.
3. Dip the chicken in egg and immediately dredge in breadcrumbs mixture. Coat well and place in the air fryer basket.
4. Place the air fryer basket in the air fryer.
5. Air fry at 180 degree C for 12-15 minutes or until golden brown. Turn the chicken around a couple of times in between.
6. Remove from the air fryer and place on a serving platter. Serve with a dip of your choice.

Lamb Roast

Ingredients:

- 1 pound lamb roast
- 1 large potato, chopped into chunks
- 1 bunch Dutch carrots, trimmed, peeled
- 1 small sweet potato, peeled, chopped into chunks
- 1 cup frozen peas, thawed, cooked
- 1 tablespoon instant gravy mix, cook according to instructions on package
- 1 tablespoon olive oil
- 2 teaspoons onion flakes
- 2 teaspoons crushed garlic
- 2 teaspoons dried rosemary
- Salt to taste
- Pepper powder to taste

Method:

1. Place carrots and potatoes on the baking accessory. Sprinkle salt and pepper.
2. Place the baking accessory in a preheated air fryer and air fry at 180 degree C for 15 minutes. When done, remove from the air fryer and set aside to keep warm.
3. Meanwhile, mix together, rosemary, oil, garlic and onion flakes in a small bowl and rub this mixture over the lamb.
4. Place a small skillet over medium heat and add lamb. Cook until lamb is brown on all sides.
5. Remove from pan and sprinkle salt and pepper.

6. Spread a sheet over foil over the baking tray and place baking paper over it. Place the browned lamb over it along with sweet potato.
7. Bake in the air fryer at 180 degree C for 20-25 minutes. Remove lamb from air fryer and place on the cutting board. When cool enough to handle, slice the lamb.
8. In case sweet potato is not cooked, bake for some more time until done.
9. Serve lamb with baked potatoes, sweet potato, carrots, cooked peas and gravy.

Lamb Chops with Garlic Sauce

Ingredients:

- 4 lamb chops
- 1 small garlic bulb
- 1/2 tablespoon fresh oregano, minced
- 1 1/2 tablespoons olive oil
- Freshly ground black pepper
- Salt to taste

Method:

1. Rub olive oil all over the garlic bulb.
2. Place the garlic bulb in the air fryer basket and place the basket in the air fryer.
3. Air fry in a preheated air fryer at 200 degree C for 12 minutes. When done, remove from the basket.
4. Mix together oregano, oil, salt, and pepper. Apply a thin layer of this mixture all over the lamb chops. Set aside for 5-7 minutes. Set aside the remaining mixture.
5. Place the lamb chops in the air fryer basket and place the basket in the air fryer.
6. Air fry in a preheated air fryer at 200 degree C for 7 minutes. When done, remove from the basket and place on a serving platter.
7. To make garlic sauce: Squeeze the garlic cloves and add to the remaining oil mixture. Season with salt and pepper. Mix well.
8. Serve lamb chops with garlic sauce.

Lamb Rump Mini Roast

Ingredients:

- 3 small potatoes, rinsed, scrubbed, halved
- 1 ¼ cup lamb rump
- 1 medium onion, halved
- 1 cup frozen sweet potato fries
- 1 tablespoon garlic paste
- 1 teaspoon olive oil
- Salt to taste
- 1 teaspoon dried rosemary

Method:

1. Mix together garlic and rosemary and rub it over the lamb rump.
2. Place a divider inside the air fryer and place lamb rump in one part of it.
3. Air fry at 180 degree C for about 40 minutes.
4. Place the sweet potatoes in the other part of it. Place potatoes and onions over the sweet potatoes.
5. Air fry at 180 degree C for 20 minutes or until vegetables are done.
6. Serve Lamb rump with the roasted vegetables.

Vegetable Lasagna

Ingredients:

- 1 pound pumpkin, peeled, finely chopped
- 3/4 pound beets, cooked, thinly sliced
- 1 pound tomatoes, chopped
- 1/2 pound fresh whole wheat lasagna sheets
- 1 medium onion, chopped
- 1 tablespoon fresh rosemary, torn
- 1 tablespoon sunflower oil or olive oil
- Goats cheese, grated as much as required

Method:

1. Toss pumpkin with 1/2 tablespoon of olive oil and place on the baking tray.
2. Place the baking tray in a preheated air fryer and bake at 175 degree C for 10 minutes. Remove from air fryer and let it cool.
3. Add pumpkin, onion, tomatoes and rosemary to a blender and blend until smooth. Alternately, blend with a hand blender.
4. Transfer into a pan and place the pan over low heat. Cook for 5-6 minutes.
5. Take a greased baking dish that fits well into the air fryer.
6. Spread some sauce at the bottom of the dish. Lay a layer of lasagna sheets so as to cover the bottom of the dish.
7. Spread 1/3 of the beet slices over the lasagna sheets and spread 1/3 of goat's cheese over the beet.
8. Spread half the sauce over the cheese layer.

9. Repeat step 6, 7 and 8 until all the ingredients are used up. Final layer should be of cheese.
10. Place the baking dish in the air fryer and bake at 150 degree C for 45 minutes.
11. Remove from air fryer and serve.

Paneer 65

Ingredients:

- 2 ½ cup paneer (a type of fresh cottage cheese found in Indian stores), chopped into cubes
- 4 tablespoons yogurt
- 1 large onion, finely chopped
- 1 teaspoon garlic paste
- 1 teaspoon ginger paste
- 2 tablespoons wheat flour
- 2 tablespoons lemon juice
- 15-20 curry leaves
- 4 tablespoons ketchup
- 6-8 green chilies
- 2 tablespoons chili sauce
- Salt to taste
- 1/2 cup oil

Method:

1. Mix together in a bowl, flour, chili powder, yogurt, ginger paste, garlic paste, lemon juice and salt.
2. Add paneer pieces and toss well. Let it marinate for at least an hour.
3. Transfer the paneer pieces into a greased baking accessory. Drizzle 2-3 tablespoons oil over it. Place the baking accessory in the air fryer.
4. Air fry in a preheated air fryer at 200 degree C for 10 minutes. Retain the marinade.
5. Meanwhile place a pan over high heat. Add a tablespoon of oil. When oil is heated, add onions,

curry leaves and green chili and sauté for a couple of minutes.

6. Add 1/2-cup water retained marinade, ketchup and chili sauce. Add air-fried paneer and heat thoroughly.
7. Remove from heat and serve hot with steamed rice.

Asian Mixed Noodles

Ingredients:

- 1/2 cup cabbage, cut into thin strips
- 1 carrot, peeled, cut into thin matchsticks
- 1 large onion, thinly sliced
- 1 green bell pepper, thinly sliced
- 4 cloves garlic, minced
- 1 small packet brown rice noodles
- 1 cup chicken, cooked, cut into small pieces
- 2 teaspoons soy sauce
- White pepper powder to taste

Method:

1. Soak the rice noodles in hot water for about 7-10 minutes and drain. Break the noodles into smaller pieces.
2. Add rest of the ingredients to the air fryer and mix well.
3. Air fry at 200 degree C for about 5 minutes.
4. Add noodles and toss well.
5. Air fry for another 8 minutes. Stir in between a couple of times.
6. Serve hot.

Hasselback Potatoes

Ingredients:

- 2 medium sized potatoes, peeled, cut a thin slice so that it can stand
- 1 medium onion, halved, sliced
- 1 steak, cut into strips
- 10 mushrooms, quartered
- 1/2 cup snow peas
- 2 tablespoons olive oil
- 1 teaspoon soy sauce
- 1/4 teaspoon salt or to taste
- 1/8 teaspoon pepper powder
- 2 teaspoons ketjap manis sauce (a thick, sweet, Indonesian soy sauce)

Method:

1. Prick the potatoes with a fork. Take about a tablespoon of oil and brush the potatoes with it. Season the potatoes with salt and pepper.
2. Place the potatoes in the baking accessory.
3. Place the baking accessory in the air fryer.
4. Air fry in a preheated air fryer at 190 degree C for 20 minutes.
5. Meanwhile mix together rest of the ingredients and marinate for a while.
6. Push the potatoes to one side and place the marinated ingredients in the middle.
7. Air fry for 5 more minutes.
8. Serve potatoes with the vegetable - steak mixture.

Falafels

Ingredients:

- 2 cups cooked chickpeas
- 1 medium onion, minced
- 2 cloves garlic, minced
- 1/4 teaspoon chili powder
- 1 green chili, finely sliced
- 1/2 teaspoon salt or to taste
- 1/2 teaspoon cumin powder
- 1/2 teaspoon coriander powder
- 2 tablespoons fresh parsley, minced
- Oil for greasing

Method:

1. Add chickpeas, chili powder, salt, cumin powder, and coriander powder to the food processor and pulse until well mashed.
2. Transfer into a bowl. Add onion, garlic, parsley and green chili. Mix well.
3. Divide into 8-9 balls and shape into patties. You can grease your palms for shaping into patties.
4. Grease aluminum foil with a little oil.
5. Place the foil in the air fryer basket. Place the air fryer basket in the air fryer
6. Air fry in a preheated air fryer at 200 degree C for 15 minutes or until golden.
7. Serve hot with ketchup or mint or cilantro chutney.

Side Dishes Recipes

Buttery Dinner Rolls

Ingredients:

- 1 1/8 cup whole wheat flour
- 1 1/8 teaspoon instant yeast
- 1/3 cup sugar
- 3/4 teaspoon salt
- 1/2 cup fresh milk at room temperature
- ¼ cup butter, softened
- 1 egg
- Melted butter to brush

Method:

1. Pour milk in the bread maker pan. Then add butter followed by sugar, egg, salt, wheat flour and yeast.
2. Select Dough option and when the dough is formed, transfer on to your work area dusted with flour and knead with your hands.
3. Lightly grease the edges of the basket. Line the air fryer basket with baking sheet.
4. Divide the dough and make 10 -12 balls. Place the balls in the basket and cover with a damp cloth. Let it rise for at least 30 minutes or until the balls have doubled in size.
5. Bake in a preheated air fryer at 160 degree C for 13 - 15 minutes. Bake in batches.
6. Brush the dinner rolls with melted butter and serve.

Onion Fried Rice

Ingredients:

- 1 cup brown rice, soaked for 30 minutes
- 1 1/2 cups water or vegetable stock
- 2 tablespoons butter
- 1 large onion, chopped
- 1 teaspoon herbs of your choice
- 1/2 teaspoon salt or to taste
- 1/4 teaspoon pepper powder (optional)

Method:

1. Place a nonstick skillet over medium heat. Add 1-tablespoon butter. When butter melts, add onions and sauté until onions are translucent.
2. Add rice and sauté for a few more minutes.
3. Transfer into the air fryer baking accessory pan. Add salt and herbs of your choice.
4. Pour water and mix.
5. Take a parchment paper and make a small hole in the center. Place the parchment paper inside the basket and cover with a foil (make a small hole in the center of the foil) or lid of your pan.
6. Air fry in a preheated air fryer at 180 degree C for about 18-20 minutes.
7. Remove from the air fryer. Add the remaining butter and stir.
8. Cover it back with parchment paper and set aside for about 10.
9. Fluff with a fork and serve.

Stuffed Okra

Ingredients:

- 1 dozen medium sized okra, cut off the tops and tails
- 1 teaspoon ginger paste
- 1 teaspoon garlic paste
- 2 tablespoons onion paste
- 1 teaspoon cumin powder
- 1 teaspoon coriander powder
- 1/2 teaspoon turmeric powder
- 1 teaspoon dry mango powder
- 1/2 teaspoon salt or to taste
- 2 tablespoons chickpea flour (garbanzo flour)
- Cooking spray

Method:

1. Mix together all the ingredients except okra in a bowl.
2. Slit the okras horizontally. Leave a cm each on either sides and leave the base intact (do not slit right till the bottom and the sides).
3. Stuff the okras with the mixture.
4. Place the stuffed okra in the baking accessory and place the baking accessory in the air fryer basket.
5. Air fry in a preheated air fryer at 180 degree C for 12 -15 minutes.
   Note: The same filling can be stuffed in tomatoes. (Slice the top of the tomatoes and deseed). The cooking time will be lesser.

Baked Potatoes

Ingredients:

- 2 tablespoons butter, softened
- 8 potatoes, peeled, halved

Method:

1. Line the air fryer basket with aluminum foil.
2. Brush the potatoes with butter and place in the air fryer basket.
3. Place the air fryer basket in the air fryer and air fry at 180 degree C for 10 minutes.
4. Brush the potatoes again with a little butter and air fry for 10 minutes. If the potatoes are not cooked, repeat this process.
5. Serve hot.

Stuffed Baked Potatoes

Ingredients:

- 2 tablespoons butter, softened
- 8 medium potatoes, peeled, halved
  For stuffing:
- 1/2 cup bacon, chopped
- 1 onion, chopped
- 2 cloves garlic, minced
- 1/4 teaspoon salt or to taste
- 1/4 teaspoon pepper powder
- 1/2 cup cheddar cheese, grated

Method:

1. Line the air fryer basket with aluminum foil.
2. Brush the potatoes with butter and place in the air fryer basket.
3. Place the air fryer basket in the air fryer and air fry at 180 degree C for 10 minutes.
4. Brush the potatoes again with a little butter and air fry for 10 minutes. Remove from the air fryer.
5. When potatoes are cool enough to handle, scoop out the inside of the potatoes and set aside the potato cases
6. Meanwhile, place a pan over medium heat. Add bacon, scooped potato, onion and garlic and sauté until the bacon is cooked.
7. Remove from heat and add half the cheese, mix well. Cool for a while.
8. When cool enough to handle, stuff this mixture inside the potato cases.

9. Place the potato cases back in the air fryer and sprinkle the remaining cheese over it.
10. Air fry for 6-8 minutes. Remove from the air fryer and serve hot.

Thai Fish Cakes with Mango Salsa

Ingredients:

- 2 ½ cup fish fillets
- 1 egg
- 2 green onions, finely chopped
- Juice of 1 1/2 limes
- Zest of 1 1/2 limes, grated
- 1/4 cup flat leaf parsley or cilantro
- 1/3 cup ground coconut
- 2 medium ripe mangoes, peeled, cut into small cubes
- 2 teaspoons red chili paste
- Salt to taste

Method:

1. Add fish, 3/4th of the lime zest, egg, salt, 1 1/2 teaspoon red chili paste, 3 tablespoons coconut and half the lime juice to the food processor and pulse until well combined.
2. Transfer into a bowl. Add cilantro and green onion. Divide the mixture into 15-18 equal portions and shape them into patties.
3. Place 5-6 fish cakes in the air fryer basket. Place the basket in the air fryer.
4. Air fry in a preheated air fryer at 200 degree C for 7 minutes until golden brown.
5. Fry the remaining fish cakes in batches.
6. Meanwhile make the mango salsa as follows: Mix together in a bowl, mango, 1 teaspoon chili paste, a

little cilantro leaves, remaining lime juice, and 1/4 of the lime zest. Mix well and set aside.

7. Serve fish cakes with mango salsa.

Sweet potato Fries

Ingredients:

- 2 large sweet potatoes, peeled, chopped into fries
- Salt to taste
- 1/2 teaspoon dried parsley
- 1 teaspoon olive oil

Method:

1. Place the sweet potatoes in a bowl of cold water for 30 minutes. Drain and pat dry with a kitchen towel.
2. Place the fries in a bowl and drizzle oil over it. Toss well.
3. Place the sweet potatoes in the air fryer basket. Air fry in a preheated air fryer at 180 degree C for 25 minutes or until done.
4. Remove from the fryer and season with salt and parsley.
5. Serve hot.

Conclusion

I thank you once again for choosing this book and hope you had a good time reading it. The main aim of this book was to educate you on the basics of an air fryer and why you should include one in your kitchen.

As is apparent, the air fryer is extremely useful and can help you prepare healthy alternatives. You won't have to worry about the calorie intake while consuming your favorite foods, as the air fryer will add only minimal calories.

I hope you have a great time cooking with your air fryer.

Happy cooking!

Made in the USA
Lexington, KY
22 September 2016